birds

OF YELLOWSTONE AND GRAND TETON NATIONAL PARKS

BY DICK FOLLETT

BOOK DESIGN & ILLUSTRATIONS by Bill Chapman

Published by

Yellowstone Library and Museum Association

in cooperation with

National Park Service
U.S. Department of Interior

contents

preface

Yellowstone and Grand Teton are national parks of unequalled natural diversity and scenic splendor. They combine the breath-taking beauty of the Teton Mountains and the Grand Canyon of the Yellowstone with the uniquely fascinating hydrothermal features of Yellowstone. They provide the visitor with almost unlimited opportunities for wildlife observation and backcountry hiking. In the vastness of the Yellowstone and Grand Teton wilderness one may find peace and solitude and a special satisfaction in observing the beauties of the landscape and the unimpaired operation of a natural ecosystem.

One of the primary sources of the vitality of this ecosystem is the birds. Among these bird residents are endangered species such as the bald eagle; rare species of limited distribution, including the black rosy finch and the great gray owl; species of elegant form or striking beauty such as the trumpeter swan and the western tanager, and species with unique adaptations, including the dipper and the sage grouse. An osprey soaring over the Grand Canyon of the Yellowstone, a family of Canada geese floating along the Yellowstone River in Hayden Valley, a gray jay stealing food scraps from a picnic table at Colter Bay, and a Clark's nutcracker along the trail to Amphitheatre Lake — these are all part of the national park experience. This booklet was prepared with the hope that it will increase your understanding and appreciation of the birds of Yellowstone and Grand Teton National Parks.

introduction

HOW TO USE THIS BOOK

About this book:

This book provides information on the descriptions, habits and ecology of sixty-four of the most common and distinctive birds of Yellowstone and Grand Teton. It also provides a habitat guide to birding and a checklist for the two parks. This book was designed to complement, rather than replace, the standard field guides. If you desire more information on park birds, inquire at the nearest museum or visitor center.

Habitat Complexes of Yellowstone and Grand Teton National Parks

Most species of birds are limited to a specific habitat by adaptations that they have made to the physical and biological conditions found within that habitat or complex. For this reason, the process of locating a particular species is greatly simplified by knowing where to look. This section was designed as a general habitat guide to the birds of Yellowstone and Grand Teton. It provides a brief physical and biological description of the habitat complexes found in the two parks and lists characteristic birds that might be found in each complex.

4

Feeding Adaptations of Yellowstone and Grand Teton Birds

Birds are widely distributed in a variety of habitats. Many species, however, are limited to a particular habitat, or even to a niche within that habitat, because they have developed feeding specializations which make them dependent on that habitat or niche. This section features illustrations of feeding adaptations of birds occupying a variety of such niches in Yellowstone and Grand Teton.

Environmental Adaptations of Yellowstone and Grand Teton Birds

In a sense, a national park is a living ecological museum chronicling the interrelationships of living things and the relationships of these living things to their environments. This section explores a few of these relationships, including the adaptations of birds to Yellowstone's hydrothermal regions.

Birds of Yellowstone and Grand Teton National Parks

This section provides information on the appearance, habits, distribution, and ecology of 64 of Yellowstone and Grand Teton's most common and most distinctive birds. A color photograph accompanies each article.

Yellowstone and Grand Teton Bird Checklist

Lists all of the species which have been observed in the two parks and provides information on their general abundance and seasonal occurrence.

bird habitat complexes

OF YELLOWSTONE AND
GRAND TETON NATIONAL PARKS

By natural selection, various species of birds have adapted to life in a variety of natural environments. Habitat requirements evolved over long periods and were influenced by factors such as geographic isolation and availability of food and cover.

Habitat requirements vary with each species. Some species adapt to a wide variety of environmental conditions, while other species have very specific requirements. Natural communities or complexes are populated by species occupying every available niche within the community. However, these environmental complexes seldom have definite boundaries. Transitional areas between these complexes often support a greater number and variety of birds than their adjacent complexes.

The ranges and habitats of birds are slowly, but continuously, undergoing changes as a result of competition and interaction with other species and other organisms (including man), natural succession and climatic changes. More than 225 species of birds have been recorded in one or more of the habitat complexes in Yellowstone and Grand Teton National Parks. The following descriptions of bird habitat complexes was designed to serve as a general guide to bird distribution in the two parks.

Lodgepole Pine/Spruce-Fir Complex

Dense stands of lodgepole pine blanket more than sixty percent of the combined area of Yellowstone and Grand Teton National Parks. In Yellowstone and in the northern portion of Grand Teton, lodgepole pine attains climax conditions in porous volcanic soils with low fertility. In the central and southern portions of Grand Teton, however, lodgepole pine grows primarily in the soils of glacial moraines. True climax is seldom reached in any of the forested communities of Yellowstone and Grand Teton, however, because of naturally recurring fire.

The regenerative growth that follows a fire, as well as the standing snags left by a fire, provide nesting sites, cover, and food sources for a variety of birds. Successional rates are slow in the Yellowstone and Northern Grand Teton lodgepole pine complexes because of marginal moisture and low fertility. Whitebark pine is thinly scattered throughout the lodgepole pine complex in Yellowstone, but is confined to mountain canyons above 8,000 feet in Grand Teton. Pockets of spruce and fir are found along stream bottoms and pond margins. Forest floor vegetation is short and sparse, consisting primarily of elk sedge, pine grass, and grouse whortleberry.

In contrast to the lodgepole pine complex, the soils of the spruce-fir complex are generally more moist and fertile. Engelmann spruce and subalpine fir are the dominant climax trees. However, lodgepole pine in various stages of succession covers a large portion of the complex. Whitebark pine grows in large stands near timberline. The forest floor vegetation of the spruce-fir complex is lush. Dominant plants include globe huckleberry, grouse whortleberry, arnica, aster, and fleabane.

Characteristic Birds of Lodgepole Pine/Spruce-Fir Complex:

goshawk, blue grouse, ruffed grouse, great gray owl, calliope humming-bird, Williamson's sapsucker, hairy woodpecker, Hammond's flycatcher, olive-sided flycatcher, gray jay, Steller's jay, common raven, Clark's nutcracker, mountain chickadee, red-breasted nuthatch, brown creeper, dipper, American robin, hermit thrush, Townsend's solitaire, ruby-crowned kinglet, yellow-rumped warbler, western tanager, Cassin's finch, pine grosbeak, pine siskin, red crossbill, dark-eyed junco, white-crowned sparrow.

Douglas-Fir/Aspen Complex

Bill Chapman

Along a broad zone between the upper edge of the sagebrush-grassland community and the lower edge of the dense lodgepole forests at elevations up to 8500 feet, scattered stands of Douglas-fir and aspen grow. The Douglas-fir, with its thick fire-resistant bark, has probably persisted in this environment because of its ability to withstand ground fires. On exposed sites it is scattered sparsely, but grows in reasonably dense stands on most drier south and west facing slopes. Aspen also occur in scattered stands in this environment, particularly where spring seepages or high water tables exist. The absence of fire for the past eighty years and heavy browsing, particularly by elk, have retarded the growth and expansion of the aspen. Limber pine appears in pockets largely confined to the Mammoth Hot Springs area in Yellowstone and is scattered generally throughout Grand Teton. Rocky Mountain and common juniper also occur in drier transitional areas within this complex. In forested areas the forest floor vegetation includes snowberry, pine grass, and a variety of wildflowers.

8

Characteristic Birds of Douglas-Fir/Aspen Complex:

Cooper's hawk, red-tailed hawk, American kestrel, blue grouse, ruffed grouse, great horned owl, common nighthawk, common flicker, yellow-bellied sapsucker, downy woodpecker, dusky flycatcher, violet-green swallow, tree swallow, black-capped chickadee, mountain chickadee, white-breasted nuthatch, red-breasted nuthatch, house wren, American robin, hermit thrush, Swainson's thrush, mountain bluebird, Townsend's solitaire, ruby-crowned kinglet, starling, yellow-rumped warbler, Mac-Gillivray's warbler, western tanager, evening grosbeak, Cassin's finch, pine siskin, green-tailed towhee, dark-eyed junco, chipping sparrow.

Sagebrush-Grassland Complex

The sagebrush-grassland communities in Yellowstone and Grand Teton are located in dry environments generally below 7500 feet. This complex is generally confined to broad valleys and plateaus which are blanketed with sagebrush. The prevalence of sagebrush may be due, in part, to past fire suppression. The groundcover in the sagebrush-grassland complex consists primarily of bluebunch wheatgrass, Idaho fescue, Junegrass, and a variety of wildflowers. Along the edges of this complex juniper, aspen, and Douglas-fir grow in scattered clusters. Pothole lakes in these areas attract many birds. In Grand Teton sagebrush complexes occur primarily on gravelly glacial soils. Several sagebrush-grassland complexes in Yellowstone occur on glacial deposits. These include Hayden Valley, Pelican Creek, portions of Lamar Valley, the upper Gardiner River drainage, an area near Lewis Lake, and the area surrounding Yellowstone Lake. In Grand Teton extensive areas of the sagebrush-grassland complex can be found over the entire valley floor.

9

Characteristic Birds of Sagebrush-Grassland Complex:

Swainson's hawk, sage grouse, sandhill crane, mourning dove, common nighthawk, horned lark, black-billed magpie, sage thrasher, western meadowlark, Brewer's blackbird, lazuli bunting, green-tailed towhee, savannah sparrow, vesper sparrow, Brewer's sparrow.

Cottonwood-Willow Streamside Complex

This habitat occurs along stream margins at lower elevations and in stream valleys at medium elevations. Dominant cover is narrowleaf cottonwood mixed with scattered stands of Douglas-fir and blue spruce-Engelmann spruce hybrids. In Grand Teton this cover includes blue spruce but not Douglas-fir. Understory plants include russet buffaloberry, silverberry, Utah honeysuckle, mountain alder, and water birch, while willows of various species and aquatic sedges grow in extensive valley bottoms and stream meanders.

Characteristic Birds of Cottonwood-Willow Streamside Complex:

great blue heron, red-tailed hawk, Swainson's hawk, bald eagle, osprey, American kestrel, spotted sandpiper, common flicker, downy woodpecker, black-billed magpie, house wren, willow flycatcher, olive-sided flycatcher, American robin, tree swallow, black-capped chickadee, Swainson's thrush, warbling vireo, yellow warbler, MacGillivray's warbler, common yellowthroat, Wilson's warbler, brown-headed cowbird, black-headed grosbeak, chipping sparrow, white-crowned sparrow, song sparrow.

Ponds, Lakes, Rivers, and Marshes Complex

Dominated by Yellowstone Lake and Jackson Lake, this complex includes numerous ponds, lakes, rivers, and marshy areas which dot the landscapes of both Yellowstone and Grand Teton National Parks. Larger rivers include the Yellowstone, Madison, and Snake. Unique aquatic areas in Yellowstone include the glacial pothole areas of the Lamar Valley and the aquatic areas associated with the hydrothermal features. The aquatic features of both parks are ringed with pondweed, pond lily, marestail, cattail, elodea, and other aquatic plants.

Characteristic Birds of Ponds, Lakes, Rivers and Marshes Complex:

white pelican, great blue heron, trumpeter swan, Canada goose, mallard, gadwall, pintail, green-winged teal, blue-winged teal, American wigeon, ring-necked duck, lesser scaup, Barrow's goldeneye, bufflehead, ruddy duck, common merganser, bald eagle, marsh hawk, osprey, sandhill crane, sora, American coot, killdeer, common snipe, spotted sandpiper, Wilson's phalarope, California gull, belted kingfisher, cliff swallow, dipper, common yellowthroat, yellow-headed blackbird, red-winged blackbird, Brewer's blackbird, savannah sparrow, song sparrow.

Alpine Complex

An area of severe environmental conditions, the alpine complex is generally found at elevations in excess of 10,000 feet in Yellowstone and Grand Teton. Extensive areas, particularly in the Tetons, consist of open cliffs and talus slopes. Vegetation at this elevation is confined to sedges, grasses, heaths, and dwarfed, ground-hugging shrubs and trees. In wetter areas the vegetation consists of alpine meadows, while drier windswept ridges are covered with mat-forming plants. In Yellowstone alpine areas are located in the higher regions of the Gallatin and Absaroka Ranges.

Characteristic Birds of Alpine Complex:

golden eagle, horned lark, common raven, Clark's nutcracker, water pipit, black rosy finch, white-crowned sparrow.

feeding adaptations

OF YELLOWSTONE AND GRAND TETON BIRDS

Through natural selection birds have developed techniques for collecting food in a variety of environmental niches. Some species collect food in a wide range of environments, while others are highly specialized. Pictured here are feeding adaptations of several Yellowstone and Grand Teton birds.

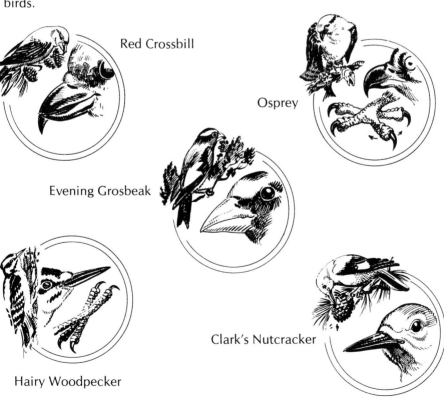

Red Crossbill

Osprey

Evening Grosbeak

Clark's Nutcracker

Hairy Woodpecker

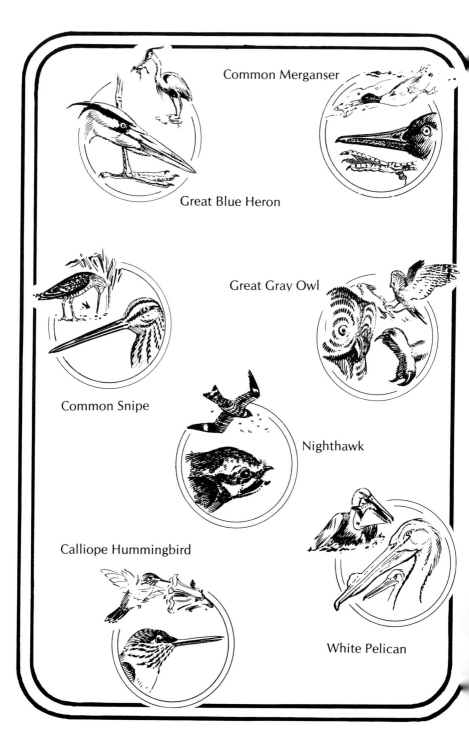

Common Merganser

Great Blue Heron

Great Gray Owl

Common Snipe

Nighthawk

Calliope Hummingbird

White Pelican

environmental adaptations

OF YELLOWSTONE AND
GRAND TETON BIRDS

(1) Several species of birds have made behavioral adaptations which allow them to live and breed in Yellowstone's thermal basins. Killdeer feed on the abundant insect life which thrives in the warm runoff channels of geysers and hot springs, and nest on the barren regions of sinter or travertine deposited by the geysers and hot springs. Woodpeckers, bluebirds, nuthatches, swallows and chickadees utilize the dead trees scalded or drowned by thermal waters for nesting sites.

(2) Man's role as a nonconsumptive user of our national parks is unique. Here wildlife populations roam freely interacting with one another as they have for centuries. In this dynamic interaction, magpies and ravens have developed an important role as scavengers, often in a symbiotic relationship with predators such as the coyote.

15

(3) Natural fires have played a major role in the development of the vegetation of Yellowstone and Grand Teton. Yet only recently has the im-
portance of fire been recognized as a factor in the natural development
of the environment. Fire suppression policies dating back to 1889 in
Yellowstone have retarded natural succession and subtly influenced
the population and distribution of several species of birds. Grouse,
woodpeckers, tree swallows, and bluebirds are particularly benefited
by periodic natural fires which provide both nesting sites and food
supplies. The presence of woodpeckers and other species help, in turn,
to maintain balances essential to any natural forest community. One
example of birds benefiting from natural fires was the dramatic increase
in three-toed woodpeckers following the fire west of Jackson Lake in
1974.

(4) The protection afforded the trumpeter swan in Yellowstone National
Park and neighboring Red Rock Lakes National Wildlife Refuge in south-
western Montana, and later in Grand Teton National Park, helped preserve this graceful, picturesque species. Fifty years ago the trumpeter
swan population had decreased to fewer than seventy. Today, largely as
a result of protection in these sanctuaries, this species is no longer con-
sidered endangered.

birds

OF YELLOWSTONE AND
GRAND TETON NATIONAL PARKS

WHITE PELICAN *(Pelecanus erythrorhynchos)*

A ponderous bird with an enlarged bill and a large bill pouch, the white pelican is a fishing specialist with a somewhat limited distribution in Yellowstone and Grand Teton. In Yellowstone, it breeds in the remote southern islands of Yellowstone Lake and is usually observed on the lake and the upper portion of Yellowstone River, while in Grand Teton it is primarily observed during spring and fall migration on or near Jackson Lake. In contrast with its cousin, the brown pelican, which dives for its fish prey, the white pelican fishes while swimming buoyantly on the surface. The enlarged pouch, approximately eighteen inches long and six inches deep in an adult bird, is employed as a fish scoop. A gregarious species, pelicans nest in colonies and share the responsibilities of rearing the young. In spite of their great size, white pelicans are efficient fliers, able to soar for hours once aloft.

White Pelican   Robert G. Gildart

17

GREAT BLUE HERON *(Ardea herodias)*

The great blue heron is a large, long-necked, long-legged wading bird with a spear-like bill which it uses to capture fish, frogs, snakes and other prey. This species, which is often incorrectly referred to as a crane, is solitary in its habits except during the breeding season. During the breeding season herons form colonies, building bulky nests and raising scrawny-looking, downy young. When perching or standing in a river or stream this large, blue-gray heron has a somewhat hunched appearance. In flight the neck is folded and the legs are held stiffly behind the body. Great blue herons are fairly common breeding residents in both Yellowstone and Grand Teton.

Great Blue Heron   C. Allan Morgan

Trumpeter Swan   Harry Engels

TRUMPETER SWAN *(Olor buccinator)*

One of the most graceful and picturesque of all birds, the trumpeter swan once bred from Alaska to Wyoming and eastward to Missouri and Indiana. Commercial demand for swan feathers during the last century drastically reduced the number of trumpeters, however, and by the early 1930's fewer than seventy birds bred in the wild. The preservation of habitat and the protection of swans in Yellowstone, in neighboring Red Rock Lakes National Wildlife Refuge, and later in Grand Teton helped preserve the species. Specialized in its breeding habitat requirements, the trumpeter swan needs shallow, quiet, fresh-water environments with a relatively stable level and marshy edges. In this environment the trumpeter swan builds a mounded nest of bulrushes, sedges, or cattails and raises a brood of up to half a dozen cygnets. The largest of the swans, the trumpeter may achieve a length of 65 inches and a wing-spread of six to nine feet. Several pairs of these elegant swans, which mate for life, breed in suitable habitats in both Yellowstone and Grand Teton National Parks.

CANADA GOOSE *(Branta canadensis)*

Among the sights and sounds of nature few are as hauntingly beautiful as a honking flock of wild geese silhouetted against a crisp autumn sky. Although the species is usually migratory, many Canada geese spend the entire winter in Yellowstone and Grand Teton. Courtship of both migratory and non-migratory birds usually begins in April. Canada geese mate for life, and both male and female share the responsibility of caring for the nest and young. During the incubation period the gander guards the female on the nest and aggressively drives intruders, including coyotes and even humans, away from the nest. Once the goslings hatch, geese feed on the shore or in open fields within commuting distance of the water. Geese graze, plucking up grass and other vegetation, or they collect food from the bottom of a stream or lake. Large numbers of Canada geese summer in Yellowstone's Hayden Valley, and at Oxbow Bend in Grand Teton, and the species is generally common on lakes and rivers of both parks.

Mallard   Bruce Pitcher

GREEN-WINGED TEAL *(Anas carolinensis)*

In the shallow water of small lakes, ponds, and streams, and in marshy areas where small streams wander aimlessly through the tall grasses, the green-winged teal floats silently or turns bottoms up in search of aquatic plants and insects. Although this teal is primarily a surface-feeder, it can dive effectively if the occasion demands. Green-winged teals frequently leave the water and travel long distances in search of food. When flushed, the teal explodes from the water without the aid of a running takeoff. The flight of the teal is swift and direct, but often features unpredictable twisting and turning maneuvers. The smallest of Yellowstone and Grand Teton ducks, the green-winged teal is a common breeding bird, and an occasional winter resident in both parks.

Canada Goose   Harry Engels

MALLARD *(Anas platyrhynchos)*

This wide-ranging species is probably the most familiar of all wild ducks. Mallards are surface-feeding fresh-water ducks which feed primarily on water plants, snails, seeds, grasshoppers, wild rice, and mosquito larvae. A hardy species, the greenhead remains in Yellowstone and Grand Teton in moderate numbers throughout the winter. An active, wary, noisy duck, the mallard constructs a simple down-lined nest among the reeds and grasses along a stream, lake, or pond edge where the female lays 8 to 15 greenish-buff eggs. The female cares for the eggs and raises the young. Shortly after breeding season the male, or drake, undergoes a complete molt, becomes flightless for a time, and acquires a protective eclipse plumage almost identical to that of the female. Mallards are abundant breeding birds in aquatic environments in both parks.

Green-winged Teal   C. Allan Morgan

LESSER SCAUP *(Aythya affinis)*

The lesser scaup is a large duck with a glossy, dull purple head, a bluish bill, and a dark breast. Its finely-flecked flanks appear white at a distance. The female is generally brown with a white mask. Scaups are expert divers with large and powerful feet. They generally breed on the borders of freshwater marshes or ponds, but are most often observed in the open water of lakes and large ponds in Yellowstone and Grand Teton. The ring-necked duck, which also occurs in both parks, resembles the lesser scaup, but has a dark back and a white ring on the bill. The lesser scaup, or "bluebill," is a common summer and occasional winter resident in both Yellowstone and Grand Teton.

Barrow's Goldeneye

Harry Engels

HARLEQUIN DUCK *(Histrionicus histrionicus)*

This handsome duck is a rare breeding resident of remote stretches of the Yellowstone and Snake Rivers and their tributaries. (Harlequins are often observed on the LeHardy Rapids of the Yellowstone River in spring and early summer). Like its namesake, the masked character of comedy and pantomime, the male harlequin is richly colored with a gaudy patterned plumage of blues, russets, blacks, and whites. The female is dusky-colored with three round spots on either side of the head. Harlequins are especially attracted to rough water. They will repeatedly fly to the beginning of a series of rapids and float to their terminus, or they will use both their wings and feet to move upstream against the swift-moving current. Harlequins feed on water insects and their larvae, small fishes and tadpoles, and acquatic plants.

22

Lesser Scaup National Park Service

BARROW'S GOLDENEYE *(Bucephala islandica)*

This handsome species is the most wide-spread duck in Yellowstone and Grand Teton National Parks. It can be found not only on the major rivers and streams of both parks, but also breeds on remote streams and ponds at virtually all elevations. The male goldeneye is beautifully marked with golden eyes, white facial crescents, purplish head, and boldly marked black and white body. The female is gray, with a white collar and a dark-brown head. Goldeneyes lay their eggs in tree holes near water, and for this reason predation on young goldeneyes by weasels, martens, and even occasionally otters is not uncommon. Many Barrow's goldeneyes remain in Yellowstone and Grand Teton throughout the winter, at which time they are joined by the common goldeneye, which also winters in the area.

Harlequin Duck Kenneth W. Fink

COMMON MERGANSER *(Mergus merganser)*

Mergansers are fish-ducks, with small heads, elongated bills, and saw-edged mandibles for catching their slippery prey. Their bodies are elongated and they are more slender than most diving ducks. Although their diet is primarily fish, they also feed on mollusks, crustaceans, water insects and their larvae, and aquatic plants. The green head of the male is less crested than the female, and often appears black. The female, with a reddish head that displays more of a crest, also has a distinct white throat. The merganser is a common breeding bird on rivers and lakes in both parks.

Goshawk (Immature)   Ian C. Tait

RED-TAILED HAWK *(Buteo jamaicensis)*

Members of the Buteo family are large, thick-bodied, broad-winged hawks. In Yellowstone and Grand Teton the red-tailed hawk is the most common and widely distributed Buteo, but may be difficult to distinguish from Swainson's hawk. In both appearance and in their general ecology, the two species are similar. The reddish tail, and the generally lighter stomach and breast area of the red-tail help to distinguish it from the Swainson's hawk. Red-tailed hawks prey primarily on small rodents, including the Uinta ground squirrel. They soar effortlessly for hours in broad, sweeping circles or sit silently on exposed perches. Red-tailed hawks inhabit a wide range of habitats in both parks. Their shrill cry is one of the distinctly wild sounds of the Yellowstone and Grand Teton wilderness.

24

Common Merganser   Alan G. Nelson

GOSHAWK *(Accipiter gentilis)*

Magnificently adapted to its role as a forest predator, the goshawk depends on both speed and stealth to capture its prey. Utilizing its short, broad wings for speed and its long tail for maneuvering, the goshawk can pursue its prey through thickly wooded areas with amazing speed and agility. The goshawk preys primarily on small birds, but its diet includes grouse, voles, shrews, mice, chipmunks, squirrels, muskrats, hares, rabbits, and marmots. The adult goshawk has a uniformly blue-gray back, a finely barred white stomach, a dark crown with a white eye stripe and red eyes. One of the handsomest and deadliest of all birds, the goshawk is secretive in its habits and is uncommon to rare in the coniferous complexes of Yellowstone and Grand Teton.

Red-tailed Hawk   Harry Engels

Bald Eagle   Kenneth W. Fink

BALD EAGLE *(Haliaeetus leucocephalus)*

It is paradoxical that the bald eagle, our national bird and long a symbol of strength and courage, is an endangered species. The increased use of pesticides and loss of habitat have combined to greatly diminish the eagle's numbers throughout the United States. Although the population density of the eagle in Yellowstone was probably never significantly higher than at present, recent studies reveal that eagle reproduction has decreased noticeably in the past two decades. The eagle's preferred habitat is near water in both parks; however, a study in Yellowstone indicated that less than half of the eagle's diet in Yellowstone is made up of fish. This study revealed that birds, primarily ducks, constituted more than half of the eagle's diet. With its pronounced white head, hooked beak, deeply-curved talons, and seven-foot wing spread, the bald eagle is truly an impressive bird. Breeding populations in Yellowstone and Grand Teton are largely confined to Yellowstone Lake and the Snake River.

26

OSPREY *(Pandion haliaetus)*

The nickname "Fish hawk" accurately describes the osprey, for its diet is made up entirely of fish. The average consumption of an adult osprey is approximately one pound a day. Magnificently adapted to this specialty, the osprey has a strong, hooked beak, excellent eyesight, and talons especially adapted to fish-catching. The talons of the osprey have sharp spines which aid the bird in grasping its prey. A conspicuous crook or bend in the wing and black wrist marks near the crook are excellent flight field marks. Research conducted in Yellowstone has revealed that human activity near nesting sites can have an adverse effect on breeding success. Ospreys are frequently observed in the Grand Canyon of the Yellowstone, along the Snake River, and over Jackson and Yellowstone Lakes.

Osprey   Harry Engels

PRAIRIE FALCON *(Falco mexicanus)*

Anyone who has observed the aerial dive of the falcon, whether as part of a mating ritual or in pursuit of prey, has witnessed one of the most thrilling and spectacular sights in the natural world. The stoop or dive of the prairie falcon may exceed 125 miles per hour. Because these magnificent birds stand at the top of the food chain and because of their popularity among falconers, both the prairie falcon and its rare counterpart, the peregrine falcon, have declined in numbers in recent decades. Streamlined, missile-shaped birds with pointed wings, prairie falcons prey primarily on smaller birds and rodents. The prairie falcon is a pale brown or sandy-colored falcon. Its most distinguishing field marks are its "dirty armpits" (distinctly dark areas in the bird's wingpits). Prairie falcons are wide ranging but show a marked preference for cliff facings. They are rare breeding inhabitants of the open cliffs and canyons of both Yellowstone and Grand Teton.

American Kestrel   Leonard Lee Rue III

BLUE GROUSE *(Dendragapus obscurus)*

The blue grouse's scientific name translates "obscure tree lover." This phrase describes well the appearance and habits of this species, for its coloration provides excellent camouflage, and it is intimately associated with conifers, particularly the Douglas-fir. The blue grouse breeds in mixed woods or open conifers, but spends the entire winter in the conifers. Conifers provide the grouse with both food and protective cover. During the mating season the male grouse or cock attracts the female with a series of booming or hooting sounds which are produced by the inflation of yellow throat sacs. The nest of the blue grouse is built on the ground, often at the base of a tree or under a fallen log. The chicks, which hatch in 26 days, develop rapidly and are able to fly efficiently in about two weeks. Blue grouse are common permanent residents of the lodgepole pine/spruce-fir and Douglas-fir/aspen complexes in both parks.

28

Prairie Falcon   Kent & Donna Dannen

AMERICAN KESTREL *(Falco sparverius)*

Although it lacks the romantic appeal of the larger and rarer falcons, the kestrel is nonetheless a handsome and interesting species. This diminutive falcon often soars leisurely. When in pursuit of prey it also kites, remaining in a stationary position in the air while surveying the landscape for insects, which are its primary prey. Both sexes have handsome black, white, blue, and reddish head and facial patterns, while the males have blue-gray wings. Kestrels are common residents of the sagebrush-grassland environments in both parks and are occasional breeders in the Douglas-fir/aspen habitat complexes. This species, which was formerly called the sparrow hawk, nests in tree cavities and cliff outcroppings. The eggs, three to seven in number, are whitish with a generally spotted appearance.

♂   ♀

Blue Grouse   Robert C. Gildart   29

RUFFED GROUSE *(Bonasa umbellus)*

The ruffed grouse is a brown or brown-red chicken-sized bird. It is a common permanent resident in both Yellowstone and Grand Teton, breeding in mixed or deciduous woods, and wintering in the conifer forests. This grouse has a broad, barred, fan-shaped tail with a black band near the tip. The mottled plumage of the ruffed grouse matches the colors and shadows of the mixed woods it inhabits. This protective coloration helps protect the grouse against natural enemies, such as the coyote. In spring, the male grouse attracts the female with a display that includes drumming. The drumming sound is produced by rapid wingbeats which compress a pocket of air against the bird's inflated chest. The varied diet of this species includes seeds, buds, foliage, nuts, wild fruits, and insects. As winter approaches, the ruffed grouse grows a series of hairlike bristles along the toes. These aid the bird in walking over snow. Grouse frequently bury themselves in snowdrifts at night. The snow provides them with warmth and protection.

Sage Grouse

Kenneth W. Fink

SANDHILL CRANE *(Grus canadensis)*

The height of a deer, this gray-brown inhabitant of marshes, meadows, and sagebrush-grassland environments is an uncommon breeding bird in both Yellowstone and Grand Teton. Cranes feed extensively on vegetable matter including bulbs, roots, grains, and berries, as well as insects, snakes, frogs, and mice. Sandhill cranes have an unusual dance which occurs most often in the spring and usually on the roosting ground. While dancing, the long legs of the crane are employed as springs and the wings are used for balance. Although the dance is used as part of a courtship display, birds of various ages participate throughout the year. The voice of the Sandhill crane is a shrill, musical rattle often uttered in flight. Bones of the Sandhill crane have been found in Pliocene and Pleistocene deposits, making it one of the oldest of all living birds.

30

Ruffed Grouse   Alan G. Nelson

SAGE GROUSE *(Centrocercus urophasianus)*

The sage grouse is an excellent example of habitat specialization, for it spends the entire year in a sagebrush environment, and the sagebrush provides the species with food, protection, and nesting cover. The sage grouse is the largest American grouse weighing up to 8 pounds. Sage grouse cocks have elaborate courtships rituals. Early in the morning, dominant males gather on display grounds where they spread their tails, droop their wings and inflate their yellow throat sacs. When the air is expelled from these sacs they produce a weak vocal sound. Males occupy territories relative to their dominance in the group. The ritualistic courtship serves not only to attract females, but also to reduce injurious fighting. Primarily a browser, the sage grouse feeds on leaves, buds, berries, and small quantities of seeds. Sage leaves are a favorite food which comprise nearly 100 percent of the bird's winter diet. Sage grouse are common in sagebrush flats of the Jackson Hole area.

Sandhill Crane   Harry Engels

31

AMERICAN COOT *(Fulica americana)*

Coots are plump, slate-gray duck-like birds with scalloped toes. They inhabit the open water of rivers and deep ponds, feeding primarily on submerged vegetation. These noisy, gregarious birds with harsh, grating calls have the curious habit of pumping their heads back and forth as they swim as if to assist in propelling themselves forward. In taking off from the water the coot requires a long running takeoff, paddling the water loudly while building up speed for the takeoff. The coot builds a floating nest which is anchored to emerging pond vegetation. The female lays a clutch of up to a dozen eggs, which are soon converted to downy, black young with red-orange heads. Coots are common on ponds, lakes, and rivers in both Yellowstone and Grand Teton National Parks.

Killdeer   Robert C. Gildart

COMMON SNIPE *(Capella gallinago)*

In the world of avian specialization, the snipe is the specialist in probing. The bill of the snipe has a flexible tip for locating and seizing its worm prey. During the mating season snipes produce a mechanical winnowing sound with their tail during a steep sky dive. This unusual mechanical sound is used in courtship and is usually performed at night or on overcast days. To produce this unusual sound, the snipe flies to a great height, then dives earthward. As it descends, air pressure against two stiff outer tail feathers cause them to vibrate, producing the winnowing sound. The snipe inhabits the borders of marshes in both Yellowstone and Grand Teton. A small, short-legged, long-billed wading bird, the snipe remains hidden until flushed and then explodes in a rapid zigzag flight pattern while uttering a raspy "scaipe" note.

32

American Coot   National Park Service

KILLDEER *(Charadrius vociferus)*

Because of their wide distribution and distinctive characteristics some birds are familiar to most everyone. The killdeer is such a bird. This handsome shorebird whose call announces its name is a member of the plover family. Killdeers do not build a nest, instead they lay their eggs on the ground in a convenient depression. For this reason their eggs and young are vulnerable to predators, as well as to human intruders. To protect the nest and young the killdeer has developed an injury-feigning distraction display. When an intruder approaches, the killdeer moves away from the eggs or young while dragging one wing, spreading the tail and uttering a loud distress call. The killdeer can be found in marshy areas throughout both parks. Many killdeers spend the entire summer in the hydrothermal environments of Yellowstone.

Common Snipe   Stephen A. Laymon

SPOTTED SANDPIPER *(Actitis macularia)*

Along the shores of ponds, lakes, rivers, and streams in both Yellowstone and Grand Teton one may encounter a small, noisy, spotted-breasted shorebird. This bird teeters nervously and when alarmed flies with stiffly held wings and short, rapid wingbeats alternated with periods of gliding. While in flight the bird utters a repetitious, staccato "peet." The well-camouflaged eggs of this species are usually placed on or near the ground along the gravelly shores of a stream or pond or within a few feet of the shore. The precocial, downy young must avoid contact with coyotes, weasels, and other forest predators if they are to grow to maturity.

California Gull   Harry Engels

MOURNING DOVE *(Zenaida macroura)*

Although it is one of the most ecologically tolerant, and therefore widely distributed of all birds, the mourning dove is a breeding bird of limited distribution in Yellowstone and Grand Teton. Because it feeds primarily on waste grains and weed seeds, the mourning dove prefers open, semi-arid environments. In Yellowstone and Grand Teton it breeds primarily in the sagebrush-grassland habitat complexes. Mourning doves construct flimsy nests of grasses or twigs. These nests are placed on any available horizontal branch. The two white eggs deposited in the nest hatch in fourteen to sixteen days. The young doves, which are fed a partly pre-digested fluid by the parents, develop rapidly, leaving the nest in twelve to fourteen days.

Spotted Sandpiper   Bruce Pitcher

CALIFORNIA GULL *(Larus californicus)*

The California gull is an opportunist that allows few sources of food to escape its notice. In Yellowstone and Grand Teton, as elsewhere, this species follows the fisherman, feeding on discarded fish and fish entrails. However, fish are but one item in a varied diet which includes mice, a variety of insects, and where available, edible parts of garbage. The adult California gull has a gray mantle with black wing tips, greenish legs, and a yellow bill with a red or red and black spot. The plumage of immature gulls reflects their age and sexual development. First-year gulls are mottled, dusky brown with flesh-colored bills, while second-year birds are pale gray. California gulls are common on larger lakes and rivers in both Yellowstone and Grand Teton.

Mourning Dove   Joe Van Wormer   35

GREAT HORNED OWL *(Bubo virginianus)*

The great horned owl is the only large North American owl with ear tufts or horns. It also has a finely barred stomach and a conspicuous white throat. Great horned owls inhabit cliffs and canyons and broken forest habitats in both parks. Their prey includes grouse, squirrels, hares and marmots, as well as small rodents and birds. Unlike most birds, owls have binocular vision. The eyeball of this owl is as large as the eye of a human, but tubular in shape. The enlarged lens-cornea portion of the eye allows it to gather and concentrate all available light. Great horned owls also have ears of unequal size which aid them in locating prey. The flight feathers of the owl's wings have finely-toothed edges which allow the bird to fly almost noiselessly. With these special adaptations, the great horned owl is truly a marvelous predator.

Great Horned Owl   Alan G. Nelson

GREAT GRAY OWL *(Strix nebulosa)*

In spite of an ever-increasing army of individuals expressing an interest in birds and the lure of the natural world, and in spite of the continued diminution of wilderness, the great gray owl remains a bird of mystery, a ghostly apparition of the deep forest. The great gray owl, like another inhabitant of the wilderness, the grizzly bear, and more than any other bird, typifies the mystique of wilderness. The most striking of all owls, the great gray owl is nearly two feet long and has a wingspread of five feet. Prominent concentric circles on facial discs are its most distinctive markings. The great gray owl flies with slow and measured wingbeats, floating noiselessly through the forest in search of its prey of mice, voles, chipmunks, and other small mammals. Great gray owls are rare inhabitants of the dense forests and adjacent meadows of Yellowstone and Grand Teton.

Great Gray Owl   Ronald L. Branson

COMMON NIGHTHAWK *(Chordeiles minor)*

The nighthawk is not a hawk at all, but a goatsucker which is adapted to aerial flycatching. Nighthawks have long wings and huge mouths. They are most active during late evening and early morning hours. In this poor light they can be identified by their unusually long wings, their erratic flight, and a nasal "peent" uttered repeatedly in flight. During the mating season nighthawks also produce an unusual booming sound which occurs when the bird initiates rapid braking wingbeats at the culmination of a spectacular aerial dive. The diet of the nighthawk is made up entirely of airborne insects which range in size from minute gnats to large moths, all of which are taken on the wing. Nighthawks are fairly common at lower elevations in both Yellowstone and Grand Teton.

Calliope Hummingbird   Danny On

BELTED KINGFISHER *(Megaceryle alcyon)*

With its harsh, rattling call, clean-cut markings and bold outline, the kingfisher is a very distinctive bird. As its name implies, the kingfisher is an excellent fisher, usually launching the attack on its prey from an exposed perch in full view of a lake or river. Kingfishers nest in holes dug in exposed banks where they lay 5 to 8 pure white eggs. The female kingfisher is distinguished from the male by a chestnut band across the breast. Several Plains Indian tribes carried kingfisher skins with them into battle, believing that the kingfisher's rapid movements were transmitted to the warrior, thus enabling him to dodge enemy bullets and arrows. In ancient England the dried body of a kingfisher was kept in the house as a protection against lightning. Kingfishers are common residents along waterways of both parks.

Common Nighthawk   Kenneth W. Fink

CALLIOPE HUMMINGBIRD *(Stellula calliope)*

In open portions of the lodgepole forest, particularly in Grand Teton, a moth-sized, green-backed hummingbird flits from flower to flower. This is the calliope hummingbird. Weighing only one-tenth of an ounce and measuring barely three inches, the calliope is the smallest of our native hummingbirds. The wingbeats of hummingbirds exceed 55 beats per second, and they alone are capable of backward flight. The calliope hummingbird occurs primarily in meadows at lower and medium elevations within the lodgepole forest. This species generally prefers red flowers and demonstrates a particular preference for gilia, monkeyflower, and paintbrush. The male calliope hummingbird is our only hummingbird with a streaked throat pattern, while the female is bronze-green above with a tinge of reddish brown on the underparts, flanks, and at the base of the tail.

Belted Kingfisher   Ian C. Tait

39

Common Flicker   Harry Engels

COMMON FLICKER *(Colaptes auratus)*

The familiar flicker is a tame, noisy bird with a variety of calls. Flickers are permanent residents of the Douglas-fir/Aspen and Cottonwood-willow streambottom habitat complexes in both Yellowstone and Grand Teton. Because of its adaptability, the flicker is generally common throughout its range. However, the pugnacious starling, an introduced species, competes with the flicker and other tree hole nesting species for nesting sites and frequently drives them from their nests. Flickers spend much of their time on the ground in search of ants, which are a primary food item. They chisel their nest cavities in dead trees, usually aspens. Because of their dependence on dead trees as nesting sites, and food sources, natural disasters such as insect infestations and fires favor woodpeckers.

Yellow-bellied Sapsucker   Dean E. Biggins

YELLOW-BELLIED SAPSUCKER *(Sphyrapicus varius)*

Sapsuckers drill rows of holes in trees and return later to collect the sap. The yellow-bellied sapsucker shows a preference for aspen and birch in Yellowstone and Grand Teton. Because these rows of holes are drilled at a slightly upward angle, they act as miniature reservoirs. The cambium underneath the bark is also a primary item in the diet of this species. Yellow-bellied sapsuckers are one of the few woodpeckers that have more vegetable matter than animal matter in their diet. In Yellowstone and Grand Teton the yellow-bellied sapsucker occurs primarily in the aspen-fir habitat complex, and it usually excavates its nest in a live aspen. The plumage of this species varies, but a narrow longitudinal white wing stripe is very distinctive in both sexes.

41

HAIRY WOODPECKER *(Dendrocopos villosus)*

Woodpeckers fill a special niche in the delicate balance of the forest community. The largest item of their diet is the larvae of wood-boring beetles. The hairy woodpecker is a valuable predator of the western pine bark beetle. Easily confused with the nearly identically marked downy woodpecker, the hairy woodpecker can be distinguished from its smaller cousin by its larger size, larger and stouter bill, and lower pitched call. Like all woodpeckers, the hairy woodpecker has a powerful neck, a bony skull and a long, slender extensible tongue. Barbs on the tip of the tongue help pull insects and grubs from burrows in the tree. Hairy woodpeckers are common residents of the lodgepole pine/spruce-fir complexes in both parks.

Hairy Woodpecker   Alan G. Nelson

42

TREE SWALLOW *(Iridoprocne bicolor)*

Tree swallows have glossy green-black backs and white underparts. Because of the abundance of aerial insects, on which they feed, they are generally widely distributed throughout both parks. However, they nest primarily in tree cavities of the aspen, in company with mountain bluebirds, flickers, house wrens, and dusky flycatchers. In their incessant pursuit of insects, tree swallows glide in wide, flat circles, darting this way and that in pursuit of their insect prey. Tree swallows are the first of their kind to arrive in spring. Following pair formation, the pair selects a hole in a tree and the female lays from four to six white eggs. The violet-green swallow, which is also common in both parks, resembles the tree swallow, but displays prominent white rump patches.

Tree Swallow   Willard E. Dilley

Barn Swallow   Bruce Pitcher

BARN SWALLOW *(Hirundo rustica)*

A handsome swallow with a blue-black back, cinnamon-buff underparts, and a deeply forked tail, the barn swallow is the epitome of grace and ease of flight. The barn swallow flies close to the ground in an undulating flight pattern. While in flight this species often utters its musical, twittering song. In Yellowstone and Grand Teton the barn swallow breeds in open meadows and marshlands. In general coloration the barn swallow resembles the cliff swallow, but the squarish tail and buffy forehead patch and underparts readily distinguish the latter species. The nest of the barn swallow is a mud cup lined with feathers. It is most often placed under a bridge or upon the side of a cliff.

GRAY JAY *(Perisoreus canadensis)*

The gray jay's long association with campers and outdoorsmen has provided the bird with a host of descriptive nicknames including "camp robber," "moose bird," "whisky jack," and "meat bird." Campers, picnickers and backcountry travelers in Yellowstone and Grand Teton are bound, sooner or later, to strike up an acquaintance with this likeable bird. Because of its loose, fluffy plumage it can fly almost noiselessly and it often glides into camp completely unnoticed. A soft whistled note may announce the arrival of a second jay. After surveying the camp and picking up any loose food morsels, the jays drift from the camp as noiselessly as they arrived. In addition to the food they scavenge from campers, and picnickers, the jay's diet fare includes berries and fruits, insects, the eggs and nestlings of other birds, and carrion. In keeping with its general character the jay's vocal repertoire is rich and varied, consisting of a great variety of squawks, screams and whistles. Gray jays are common in both Yellowstone and Grand Teton.

Black-billed Magpie   Joe Van Wormer

COMMON RAVEN *(Corvus corax)*

Ravens are intelligent, wary, adaptable birds. One of the first birds mentioned in early history and mythology, the raven was mentioned in the Biblical account of Noah's Ark and was honored as the hero-bird of the Cherokee Indians. The raven is distinguished from its cousin, the crow, which is rare in Yellowstone and Grand Teton, by its larger size, stouter bill, wedge-shaped tail, and coarser voice. The raven's diet includes small rodents and young rabbits, insects, worms, nestling birds, bird eggs, snakes, frogs, and carrion including dead elk, deer, and bison. Ravens are excellent fliers, performing a variety of flight maneuvers, including acrobatic feats and spectacular dives. Ravens are common breeding birds in both Yellowstone and Grand Teton. They prefer open terrain and canyons with steep cliffs upon which they can build their nests.

Gray Jay

Danny On

BLACK-BILLED MAGPIE *(Pica pica)*

In both personality and appearance, the magpie is a distinctive bird. Noisy, intelligent and wary, the magpie is striking in appearance with its contrasting black and white plumage and long, wedge-shaped tail. Confined to lower elevation sagebrush-grassland habitats in Yellowstone and Grand Teton, the magpie is a scavenger which profits not only from the presence of the coyote and other predators, with which it frequently associates, but also from road kills of squirrels and other rodents by the vehicles of park visitors. The magpie spends much of its time on the ground in search of food. It walks with a jerky gait or hops on both feet. The nest of this species is usually built in a dense, thorny shrub or tree. It is a large, domed mass of sticks with entrances on each side.

Common Raven

Dick Follett

CLARK'S NUTCRACKER *(Nucifraga columbiana)*

The nutcracker is a handsome, curious bird, which seems to incorporate in form or in manner the characteristics of the crow, the woodpecker, and the jay. More than any other bird, this noisy, good-natured mountaineer symbolizes the high country. Drawn to the hiker by its limitless curiosity, the nutcracker utters its harsh, grating call as if to remind the hiker that he is not alone in the wilderness. The nutcracker derives its name from the fact that it is very adept at extracting pine nuts from cones. The bird accomplishes this by employing its long bill in the fashion of a pick and a crowbar. When pine nuts are out of season, the nutcracker varies its diet with ants, beetles, grasshoppers, moths, grubs, and butterflies, which are caught both on the ground and in the air. Nutcrackers are common in both Yellowstone and Grand Teton. However, fluctuations in seed crops can dramatically affect the population of these birds from year to year.

Mountain Chickadee   Willard E. Dilley

MOUNTAIN CHICKADEE *(Parus gambeli)*

Chickadees are tame, friendly, hyperactive birds. They are constantly on the move, searching among the twigs, foliage, and bark for caterpillars, plant lice, and insect eggs. Even in bitterly cold weather, small flocks of chickadees flit among the conifers undaunted by the weather. The mountain chickadee, more common at higher elevations than its counterpart, the black-capped chickadee, is distinguished from the latter by a narrow white line which interrupts the black cap, running from the bill over and behind the eye. These agile, acrobatic birds nest in cavities in rotten stumps, laying 7 to 9 spotted eggs and raising as many as 2 or 3 broods each summer. The Cheyenne and Blackfeet Indians, which occupied or traversed much of the country in and around what has become the Yellowstone and Grand Teton Parks, revered the chickadee and referred to it as "the bird that tells us that summer is coming."

46

Clark's Nutcracker   Dick Follett

Red-breasted Nuthatch   Dean E. Biggins

RED-BREASTED NUTHATCH *(Sitta canadensis)*

The nuthatch is a small bird with a long, slightly upward-turned bill and short legs set far back on its stubby body. Unlike other birds which patrol the tree trunks, the nuthatch moves about without the aid of its tail. Furthermore, the red-breasted nuthatch not only moves laterally and upward, it also may be seen crawling down a tree trunk in jerky, circular spirals. This species feeds largely on bark insects and their larvae. It varies its diet with seeds and nuts. The nuthatch nests in a hole in a dead conifer or conifer snag, and displays the unique ability of flying directly into the nest cavity. The call of the red-breasted nuthatch is a nasal, oft-repeated "ank," which resembles the sound produced by a little tin horn. Red-breasted nuthatches breed in relatively open stands of lodgepole pine and Douglas-fir in Yellowstone and Grand Teton.

DIPPER *(Cinclus mexicanus)*

Dippers are plump, stubby-tailed, slate gray songbirds which have adopted many of the habits of the wading and diving birds. They inhabit clear, cascading mountain streams, feeding on aquatic insects. With their strong legs, special oil glands, and dense plumage, dippers are uniquely adapted to this watery habitat. Dippers have a peculiar habit of bobbing up and down, most often from a spray-drenched rock. When under water, the dipper walks along the stream bottom with the aid of its wings, feeding on water beetles, caddisflies, dragonflies, and other water-dwelling insects and their larvae. The song of the dipper is bubbling and wren-like, and its nest is a domed structure, constructed of grasses and mosses and lined with leaves and rootlets. It is usually placed near water on a rock, under a bridge, or on a ledge behind a waterfall. Dippers are common breeding birds along mountain streams in both Yellowstone and Grand Teton.

American Robin   Leonard Lee Rue III

SWAINSON'S THRUSH *(Catharus ustulatus)*

Thrushes are inconspicuous birds which spend much of their time on the ground. The Swainson's thrush is a uniformly brown bird with a spotted breast, and a buffy face and eye-ring. The hermit thrush, which is also common in Yellowstone and Grand Teton, can be distinguished from the Swainson's thrush by its reddish tail. The Swainson's thrush prefers damp areas near water, and may be found in willow thickets, river woods or forest undergrowth. It shows a particular preference for environments where conifers are mixed with aspen. To truly appreciate the thrush one must hear its song, for thrushes are among the most gifted of all songsters. To hear the song at its best, one must retreat to a cool, quiet hillside during the freshness of early morning or in the tranquil stillness of early evening, when the sun casts shafts of slanted light through the trees. In this setting, the thrush pours out its serene, flute-like song, which some consider the most beautiful sound in all of nature.

Dipper

National Park Service

AMERICAN ROBIN *(Turdus migratorius)*

The robin, with its cheery song, distinctive red-orange breast, and trusting habits, is perhaps the best known and best loved of all our native song birds. Because of its adaptability the robin thrives in almost any environment. In Yellowstone and Grand Teton the robin is one of the most abundant breeding birds, breeding in virtually every environmental complex below timberline. Robins which breed in developed areas of the parks are as tame and trusting as the robins found in towns, city parks, and farmyards; however, the backcountry hiker will encounter a wild robin whose temperament is more in keeping with its wild surroundings. The nest of the robin is grass-lined and mud-walled and the eggs are a beautiful turquoise blue.

Swainson's Thrush

Alan G. Nelson

49

MOUNTAIN BLUEBIRD *(Sialia currucoides)*

The male mountain bluebird is a striking bird with sky-blue or azure plumage and light underparts. The female is a dull brownish-gray with a touch of blue on the rump, tail and wings. The Pima Indians believed that the mountain bluebird was originally an unlovely gray, but that it acquired its present exquisite azure coat by bathing in a certain lake of blue water that had neither inlet nor outlet. The distribution and abundance of bluebirds in Yellowstone and Grand Teton is apparently influenced to some degree by the availability of nesting sites which are largely confined to dead trees in forest clearings. Lightning fires, epidemics of wood-boring insects, and similar natural agents, including the drowning or scalding of trees by hydrothermal features, are therefore beneficial to the species. The mountain bluebird is generally common in both Yellowstone and Grand Teton.

Townsend's Solitaire   Dale & Marian Zimmerman

WARBLING VIREO *(Vireo gilvus)*

The warbling vireo is a plain, sluggish dweller of the forest canopy. Showing a decided preference for decidous trees, the warbling vireo is more easily detected by song than by sight. The song is a repetitious, rolling warble. The male sings incessantly throughout the summer. The warbling vireo may be distinguished from other small residents of the forest canopy by the heavy bill and the lack of wing bars. Vireos feed almost exclusively on insects. They are especially fond of small caterpillars and measuring worms. The nest of the warbling vireo is a neat, compact cup composed of bark fibers, fine grasses, and plant stalks, ornamented with spider egg cases, lichens, and cottonwood down. The nest is usually attached to the fork of two branches, high in a deciduous tree. The tree most commonly used for nesting in Yellowstone and Grand Teton is the narrow-leaf cottonwood.

50

Mountain Bluebird   Joe Van Wormer

TOWNSEND'S SOLITAIRE *(Myadestes townsendi)*

A quiet, retiring bird, the Townsend's solitaire is a close relative of the thrushes, though it acts very much like a flycatcher. A slim, gray bird, the solitaire shows pale patches in the wings and tail in flight. Sparsely distributed through its range, the solitaire shows a marked preference for open forests of pine and fir or juniper. The nest of the solitaire, a roughly constructed mass of bark, twigs, stalks, and grasses, is usually placed on or near the ground. The eggs are white and heavily blotched with various shades of brown. This slender, long-tailed bird is most often observed perched erectly on the outermost or top-most branch of a small tree along the edge of a forest clearing. The most common call note uttered by the solitaire is a single pipping note.

Warbling Vireo   Willard E. Dilley

51

YELLOW WARBLER *(Dendroica petechia)*

The yellow warbler breeds in streamside thickets of willow, alder, and cottonwood in Yellowstone and Grand Teton. This slender, active bird is the only yellow warbler with spots on its tail. The male also has rusty streaks on the breast. The nest of the yellow warbler is a deep, felted cup placed in the upright crotch of a shrub or tree. Yellow warbler nests are frequently parasitized by cowbirds, which do not build nests of their own, but lay their eggs in the nests of other species. The larger, more aggressive cowbird fledgling usually crowds the young warblers out of the nest and becomes the sole object of the parent warbler's attention. It is not uncommon to see an adult yellow warbler feeding a cowbird fledgling twice its size.

Yellow-rumped Warbler   Dale & Marian Zimmerman

WESTERN MEADOWLARK *(Sturnella neglecta)*

The familiar meadowlark is one of our most widespread and most abundant songbirds. Its cheery song, plump profile, and conspicuously marked yellow and black breast are its most identifiable characteristics. Meadowlarks are common breeding birds in the sagebrush-grassland habitat complexes in Yellowstone and Grand Teton. In this environment the meadowlark builds a grass domed nest and feeds on beetles, crickets, grasshoppers, caterpillars, wasps, ants, spiders, and seeds. When on the ground the meadowlark flicks its tail incessantly and in flight displays white outer tail feathers. Meadowlarks are not true larks but are related to the blackbirds and orioles.

Yellow Warbler   Ian C. Tait

YELLOW-RUMPED WARBLER *(Dendroica coronata)*

The yellow-rumped warbler is the most widely distributed and most abundant western warbler. This species is always on the move, darting and flitting around twigs and branches, sometimes hanging upside down, and sometimes flycatching. The most common call uttered by this species is a metallic "chip," however, during the breeding season it sings a sweet and melodious "chee-chee-chee-ah-wee" song. The yellow throat and rump of the male are conspicuous field marks, though both fade to a faint wash in the bird's winter plumage. The yellow-rumped warbler prefers mixed woods, but usually chooses an evergreen to nest in. This species is common in both Yellowstone and Grand Teton.

Western Meadowlark   Bruce Pitcher

YELLOW-HEADED BLACKBIRD *(Xanthocephalus xanthocephalus)*

In springtime, marshes and ponds in Yellowstone and Grand Teton resound with a medley of bird calls. Coots, ruddy ducks, diving ducks, rails, yellowthroats, marsh wrens, and blackbirds all join in the annual competition for mates and territory. One of the most striking bird inhabitants of this marshland environment is the male yellow-headed blackbird. The yellow head, neck, and chest, and the broad, white wing patch contrast sharply with the black of the bird's body and tail. The male is most often seen perched in a conspicuous spot along the edge of a pond. From this location he utters a variety of harsh, unmusical notes and flits combatively through the marsh defending his territory. The female is brownish with a wash of yellow on the breast and with a white throat and streaked lower breast. This species breeds in localized colonies throughout Yellowstone and Grand Teton.

Western Tanager   Joe Van Wormer

EVENING GROSBEAK *(Hesperiphona vespertina)*

The evening grosbeak is a handsome bird with a richly colored plumage and a powerful beak. The male is yellow with black wings and tail, while the female is gray with black wings and tail. Both sexes have large white wing patches, and the female has a yellowish cast across her back and upper breast and white in her tail. During the breeding season evening grosbeaks feed primarily on conifer seeds and wild berries. When the breeding season has been completed evening grosbeaks congregate in areas where they can feed upon the ripening chokecherries. During the winter flocks of evening grosbeak descend to lower elevations to feed on the seeds of seed-bearing trees such as the box elder. It is at this time that the grosbeaks powerful beak comes into play. The powerful, overlapping mandibles are used for shearing seeds off the trees. Evening grosbeaks are fairly common permanent residents in both parks.

Yellow-headed Blackbird   Bruce Pitcher

WESTERN TANAGER *(Piranga ludoviciana)*

Amid the breathtaking beauty of the natural landscapes of Yellowstone and Grand Teton, it is most fitting that the striking western tanager should reside as one of the most common breeding birds, for it is one of the most beautiful of all birds. From a pinnacle or bough of an evergreen tree, the tanager sings its deliberate, robin-like song and on medium-height branches builds its shallow, saucer-shaped nest. The brilliant male is lemon yellow, with black wings and tail and a red head. The female is dull greenish above, yellow below, with white or yellowish wingbars. Tanagers are birds of the forest canopy. They move deliberately in their incessant search for insects, which make up the main part of their diet. Western tanagers are common breeding birds in open conifers and mixed forests of the spruce-fir, lodgepole pine and Douglas-fir/aspen habitats.

Evening Grosbeak   Dean E. Biggins

55

CASSIN'S FINCH *(Carpodacus cassinii)*

The preferred habitat of the Cassin's finch is open forest and forest edge. A common breeding bird in both parks, the Cassin's finch has a varied, liquid, warbling song. The male Cassin's finch has a brilliant red crown patch which contrasts sharply with its brownish neck. Females have narrowly striped underparts, and both sexes have unusually long wings. Like other finches, this species has a short, stout bill adapted to seed-cracking. The food of this species consists primarily of seeds, insects, and small fruits. Following pair formation in the spring, finches build a cup nest on the limb of a conifer and the female lays four or five blue, spotted eggs. In winter most Cassin's finches in Yellowstone and Grand Teton migrate to lower elevations outside the parks.

Pine Grosbeak   Harry Engels

PINE GROSBEAK *(Pinicola enucleator)*

The pine grosbeak is a relatively uncommon breeding bird of the conifer forests of Yellowstone and Grand Teton. The nest of this species is a loose cup in a low conifer branch along the edge of a stand of conifers. Our largest and one of our handsomest finches, the pine grosbeak is a hardy species with an attractive plumage and a beautiful song. Adult males have a rose-red plumage, while females and immature males are gray with a dull yellowish-tinged head and rump. Both sexes display distinct white wing bars. The powerful bill of this large finch is used to extract and crush pine seeds. The diet of this species also includes needle buds, fruits, berries, and an occasional insect. In flight the pine grosbeak has a deep, undulating flight pattern.

56

Cassin's Finch   Dale & Marian Zimmerman

Black Rosy Finch   Harold R. Holt

BLACK ROSY FINCH *(Leucosticte atrata)*

Uniquely adapted to the alpine environment, the black rosy finch is the most characteristic bird of the alpine regions of both Yellowstone and Grand Teton. Its unique adaptations include long, pointed wings for coping with the strong winds at these high elevations and a pair of pockets in the floor of the mouth, which develop during the breeding season and apparently allow the species to carry larger quantities of food on each trip back to the nest. Black rosy finches glean seeds and insects from snowfields above timberline. Rosy finches are dark sparrow-sized birds with a pinkish wash on their wings and rump and a light gray patch on the back of the head. The nest is a carefully concealed grass cup placed in a rock crevice.

57

PINE SISKIN *(Spinus pinus)*

Siskins are noisy, gregarious birds with a nomadic nature. They may be abundant some years, and scarce in others. In many ways these small, tame, streaked birds with yellow in their wings and at the base of their tails resemble their close relatives, the goldfinches. While in flight, siskins utter light, twittering notes in rhythm with their undulating flight, while at other times their notes are wheezy. Siskins breed chiefly in coniferous forests and are generally common throughout both Yellowstone and Grand Teton. In the summer their food is made up of insects, buds, small leaves, dandelion seeds, and the seeds of conifers. The nest of a siskin is usually found in a conifer. It is a compact and well-constructed cup made of dry roots, grasses, and leaves.

Red Crossbill   Dean E. Biggins

GREEN-TAILED TOWHEE *(Chlorura chlorura)*

The green-tailed towhee is a slender, long-tailed sparrow found chiefly in the low brush of open mountain sides or high sagebrush plains. The best evidence of this shy bird's presence is often its peculiar cat-like mew note, but it also possesses a rich, varied song. When flushed from a perch or hiding place, this species flies close to the ground, pumping its tail while in flight. Like other towhees, the green-tailed towhee spends much of its time on the ground scratching for insects and seeds beneath shrub or bush. This it accomplishes by hopping and then kicking backward with both feet. The green tail for which the species is named is less distinctive than its rufous cap or its white chin. Green-tailed towhees breed primarily on brushy, transitional hillsides in both Yellowstone and Grand Teton.

58

Pine Siskin   Dean E. Biggins

RED CROSSBILL *(Loxia curvirostra)*

The unique overlapping mandibles of the crossbill are used for extracting seeds from the cones of conifers. This the crossbill accomplishes by inserting the closed bill into the side of the cone and then opening the mandibles with a movement which tears out the scales and leaves the seeds exposed. Crossbills often hang from evergreen cones in the manner of a chickadee, while noisily extracting seeds with their peculiar bills. Red crossbills are vagrants, which may be abundant one year and virtually absent from the same general area the following year. The male red crossbill is brick red with a bright rump area. The female is dull olive-gray, and juveniles are streaked above and below. Red crossbills are inhabitants of the lodgepole pine/spruce-fir and Douglas fir/aspen complexes of both Yellowstone and Grand Teton.

Green-tailed Towhee   Kent & Donna Dannen

SAVANNAH SPARROW *(Passerculus sandwichensis)*

Small, shy, and lacking distinguishing markings, the savannah sparrow is easily overlooked. A heavily streaked sparrow with a narrow, yellowish streak over the eye, this species inhabits areas of short grasses or sparse vegetation, and the grassy fringes of marshes. The savannah sparrow usually remains on or near the ground, and the best evidence of its presence is often its weak, lispy song. When flushed, the savannah sparrow flies a short distance before disappearing back into the grasses. The nest of this species is a simple, grass-lined hollow on the ground. Savannah sparrows are common breeding birds in both Yellowstone and Grand Teton.

Savannah Sparrow   Stephen A. Laymon

Dark-eyed Junco   Dean E. Biggins

DARK-EYED JUNCO *(Junco hyemalis)*

The junco is one of the most abundant breeding birds in the two parks, and its abundance seems to be related to its general adaptability. Juncos are primarily birds of the open forest or of clearings in dense forests. The song of the junco is a bell-like trill. As the snows begin to melt exposing patches of bare ground, the trilling of the junco, and the emergence of the glacier lily are harbingers of spring in the forests of Yellowstone and Grand Teton. The simple, grass-lined nest of the junco is placed on the ground, often under a small conifer. Distinctive field marks of this small, active, ground-dwelling species are its light pink bill, gray or black hood, and white outer tail feathers. There are several races of juncos, and hybridization is common.

CHIPPING SPARROW *(Spizella Passerina)*

The chipping sparrow is a small, tame sparrow with a rusty cap and a black line through the eye. It inhabits open areas in relatively dry environments with thinly scattered trees. Although it occurs in several habitat types, it is most common in the fir-aspen complex. The chipping sparrow's song consists of a series of rapid, monotonous chips. The song is most often delivered from the outermost tip of a conifer branch. The nest of this species is a neat, hair-lined cup, most often built on the branch of a conifer. The eggs are light blue, richly flecked with rust. Chipping sparrows are common breeding residents in both Yellowstone and Grand Teton.

Chipping Sparrow
Willard E. Dilley

White-crowned Sparrow
Joe Van W

WHITE-CROWNED SPARROW *(Zonotrichia leucophrys)*

This handsome sparrow with a distinctive black and white crown striping is primarily a bird of the willow thickets of mountain meadows and lakes in Yellowstone and Grand Teton. The song of this species is a series of beautifully whistled notes followed by buzzing trills. When distressed, the white-crown utters a metallic "pink." Immature white-crowned sparrows have brown head stripings and pinkish bills. The nest of this species is a well-lined cup of grasses placed on the ground or in the fork of a low willow or conifer. The eggs are spotted and blue-green. This species is one of the most common breeding birds in Yellowstone and Grand Teton.

62

A checklist OF birds

OF YELLOWSTONE and GRAND TETON NATIONAL PARKS

Seasonal Status
S—March-May
S—June-August
F—September-November
W—December-February

Status of Abundance
a—abundant
c—common
lc—locally common (common in local or regional habitats within the parks)
o—occasional
r—rare
x—accidental

YELLOWSTONE					GRAND TETON			
S	S	F	W		S	S	F	W
				Loons:				
r	r	r		Common Loon	r		r	
				Grebes:				
				Red-necked Grebe	x			
		o		Horned Grebe	r	r	r	
r	r	o		Eared Grebe	r	r	o	
r		r		Western Grebe	r		r	
o	o	o		Pied-billed Grebe		r	o	
				Pelicans:				
lc	lc	o		White Pelican	lc	r	o	
				Cormorants:				
o	o			Double-crested Cormorant	r		r	
				Herons and Bitterns:				
c	c	c	r	Great Blue Heron	c	c	c	r
x				Common Egret	x			
	r			Snowy Egret		x		
r	r	r		Black-crowned Night Heron	x			
r	r	r		American Bittern	o	o	o	
				Storks and Ibises:				
x				Wood Stork				
x				White-faced Ibis	x			
				Waterfowl:				
o		o		Whistling Swan	x		x	
o	o	o	lc	Trumpeter Swan	c	c	c	lc
c	c	c	c	Canada Goose	c	c	c	c
r		r		Snow Goose	r		r	
a	c	a	c	Mallard	a	c	a	c
x				Black Duck				
c	o	c	r	Gadwall	c	o	c	r

63

c	o	c	r	Pintail	c	o	c	o
c	o	c	o	Green-winged Teal	c	o	c	o
o	o	o	r	Blue-winged Teal	o	o	o	
o	o	o		Cinnamon Teal	o	o	o	
c	o	c	o	American Wigeon	c	o	c	r
o	o	o		Northern Shoveler	r	r	r	r
	r	r		Wood Duck		r	r	
r	r	o		Redhead	r	o	c	
o	o	o	r	Ring-necked Duck	o	o	o	o
r		r		Canvasback			r	
c	c	o	r	Lesser Scaup	o	r	o	r
o				Common Goldeneye	o			o
c	c	c	o	Barrow's Goldeneye	c	c	c	o
o	o	o	o	Bufflehead	o	r	o	o
o	o	o		Harlequin Duck	r	r	r	
x		x		Black Scoter				
o	o	o		Ruddy Duck		r	r	
r	r	r	r	Hooded Merganser	r	r		r
c	c	c	c	Common Merganser	c	c	c	c
r		r		Red-breasted Merganser	r			

Vultures, Hawks and Falcons:

r	r			Turkey Vulture	x	x	x	
o	o	o	o	Goshawk	c	c	o	o
r	r	r		Sharp-shinned Hawk	o	o	o	
r	r	r		Cooper's Hawk	o	o	o	
c	c	c		Red-tailed Hawk	c	c	c	
c	c	c		Swainson's Hawk	c	c	c	
r	r	o	o	Rough-legged Hawk		r	c	c
r	r	r		Ferruginous Hawk	r	r	r	r
o	o	o	o	Golden Eagle	o	o	o	o
o	o	o	lc	Bald Eagle	o	o	o	lc
o	o	o	r	Marsh Hawk	c	c	c	r
c	c	c		Osprey	c	c	c	r
r	r	r		Prairie Falcon	o	o	o	r
r	r	r		Peregrine Falcon		r	r	r
r	r	r		Merlin	r	r	r	
c	c	c		American Kestrel	c	c	c	

Gallinaceous Birds:

c	c	c	c	Blue Grouse	o	o	o	o
r	r	r	r	Spruce Grouse				
o	o	o	r	Ruffed Grouse	c	c	c	c
r	r	r	r	Sage Grouse	lc	lc	lc	o
r	r	r	r	Gray Partridge				

Cranes:

x		x		Whooping Crane				
o	o	o		Sandhill Crane	o	o	o	

Rails and Coots:

				Virginia Rail			x	
o	o	o		Sora	o	o	o	
c	c	c		American Coot	o	o	o	r

Plovers:

				Semipalmated Plover	r		r	
c	c	c		Killdeer	c	c	c	r
r		r		Mountain Plover				
				Black-bellied Plover	r		r	

				Species				
Shorebirds:								
c	c	c	r	Common Snipe	c	c	c	r
r	r			Long-billed Curlew	o	o		
c	c	c		Spotted Sandpiper	c	c	c	
	r	r		Solitary Sandpiper		r	r	
r		r		Willet			r	
	r	r		Greater Yellowlegs		r	r	
r	r	r		Lesser Yellowlegs	r	r	r	
		r		Pectoral Sandpiper			r	
		r		Baird's Sandpiper			r	
		r		Least Sandpiper			r	
				Dunlin	x			
				Long-billed Dowitcher			r	
				Stilt Sandpiper	r			
				Semipalmated Sandpiper	x	x		
		r		Western Sandpiper			o	
r		r		Marbled Godwit	r		r	
x				Hudsonian Godwit				
o		o		Sanderling	x		x	
o	r	o		American Avocet	o	r	o	
Phalaropes:								
o	o	o		Wilson's Phalarope	o		o	
r		r		Northern Phalarope	x		x	
Jaegers:								
				Parasitic Jaeger	x	x		
Gulls and Terns:								
				Herring Gull		x		
c	c	c		California Gull	c	c	c	
	o	o		Ring-billed Gull			r	
o	r			Franklin's Gull		o		
r				Bonaparte's Gull	r			
r	r	r		Common Tern				
r	r			Caspian Tern	r	r		
r	r	r		Black Tern	r	r	r	
Doves and Cuckoos:								
				Band-tailed Pigeon	x			
o	o	o		Mourning Dove	o	o	o	
				Yellow-billed Cuckoo		x		
	x			Black-billed Cuckoo		x		
Owls:								
r	r	r	r	Screech Owl	r	r	r	r
o	o	o	o	Great Horned Owl	o	o	o	o
			x	Snowy Owl				
r	r	r	r	Hawk Owl				
r	r	r	r	Pygmy Owl	o	o	o	o
r		r		Burrowing Owl	r		r	
	x			Barred Owl				
o	o	o	o	Great Gray Owl	o	o	o	o
r	r	r		Long-eared Owl	r	r	r	
o	o	o	r	Short-eared Owl	o	o	o	r
	r	r	r	Boreal Owl			x	
r		r	r	Saw-whet Owl	r		r	r
Nighthawks:								
				Poor-will	r	r		
o	o	o		Common Nighthawk	c	c	c	

Swifts and Hummingbirds:

				Species				
x				Black Swift				
o	o	o		White-throated Swift		x		
				Black-chinned Hummingbird	r	r		
r	r			Broad-tailed Hummingbird	o	o		
r	r			Rufous Hummingbird	o	o		
r	r			Calliope Humingbird	c	c		

Kingfishers:

				Species				
o	o	o	r	Belted Kingfisher	o	o	o	r

Woodpeckers:

				Species				
c	c	c	o	Common Flicker	c	c	c	r
				Acorn Woodpecker		x		
r	r	r		Lewis Woodpecker	r	r	r	
lc	lc	lc		Yellow-bellied Sapsucker	c	c	c	
r	r	r		Williamson's Sapsucker	o	o	r	
c	c	c	c	Hairy Woodpecker	c	c	c	c
o	o	o	o	Downy Woodpecker	c	c	c	c
r	r	r	r	Black-backed Three-toed Woodpecker				
o	o	o	r	Northern Three-toed Woodpecker	r	r	r	

Flycatchers:

				Species				
o	o	o		Eastern Kingbird	o	o	o	
o	o			Western Kingbird		o		
	x			Ash-throated Flycatcher				
r	r			Say's Phoebe	r	r		
o	o	o		Willow Flycatcher	c	c	c	
o	o	o		Hammond's Flycatcher	c	c	c	
o	o	o		Dusky Flycatcher	o	o	o	
r	r			Western Flycatcher				
r	r			Western Wood Pewee	c	c		
o	o	r		Olive-sided Flycatcher	c	c		

Larks:

				Species				
c	o	o	o	Horned Lark	c	o	o	o

Swallows:

				Species				
c	c	r		Violet-green Swallow	o	o		
c	c	o		Tree Swallow	c	c	o	
r	r			Bank Swallow	c	c		
o	o			Rough-winged Swallow	c	c		
o	o	o		Barn Swallow	o	o	r	
a	a	o		Cliff Swallow	a	a		

Crows, Magpies and Jays:

				Species				
c	c	c	c	Gray Jay	a	a	a	a
o	o	o	o	Steller's Jay	c	c	c	c
lc	lc	lc	lc	Black-billed Magpie	a	a	a	a
c	c	c	c	Common Raven	a	a	a	a
r	r	r	r	Common Crow	r	r	r	r
r	r	r		Pinon Jay	r	r	r	
c	c	c	c	Clark's Nutcracker	c	c	c	c

Chickadees:

				Species				
r	r	r	r	Black-capped Chickadee	c	c	c	c
c	c	c	c	Mountain Chickadee	c	c	c	c

Nuthatches:

				Species				
o	o	o	o	White-breasted Nuthatch	c	c	c	c
c	c	c	c	Red-breasted Nuthatch	o	o	o	o
		r	r	Pygmy Nuthatch				

				Creepers:				
o	o	o	r	Brown Creeper	c	c	o	o
				Dippers:				
c	c	c	c	Dipper	c	c	c	c
				Wrens:				
o	o	o		House Wren	o	o	o	
r	r			Long-billed Marsh Wren	o	o		
lc	lc			Rock Wren	r	r		
				Thrashers:				
r	r			Catbird	r	r		
r	r			Sage Thrasher	c	c		
				Thrushes:				
a	a	a	r	American Robin	a	a	a	r
c	c	o		Hermit Thrush	c	c	r	
o	o	r		Swainson's Thrush	c	c	r	
r	r	r		Veery				
c	c	o		Mountain Bluebird	a	a	o	
o	o	o	o	Townsend's Solitaire	c	c	o	o
				Kinglets:				
r	r	r		Golden-crowned Kinglet	r	r	r	r
c	c	c		Ruby-crowned Kinglet	o	c	o	
				Pipits:				
o	o	c		Water Pipit	c	c	c	
				Waxwings:				
		o	o	Bohemian Waxwing	o			r
r	r			Cedar Waxwing	o	o	o	
				Shrikes:				
o		c	o	Northern Shrike	o		c	r
	o			Loggerhead Shrike		o		
				Starlings:				
lc	lc	lc	o	Starling	c	c	c	r
				Vireos:				
	r			Solitary Vireo		r		
	r			Red-eyed Vireo		r		
c	c	o		Warbling Vireo	a	a	o	
				Warblers:				
	x			Tennessee Warbler				
o	o	o		Orange-crowned Warbler	o	o	o	
	x			Nashville Warbler		x		
c	c	o		Yellow Warbler	a	a	c	
	x			Cape May Warbler				
c	c	c		Yellow-rumped Warbler	a	a	c	
r	r			Townsend's Warbler		o		
	x			Blackpoll Warbler				
r	r			Northern Waterthrush	r	r		
o	o	o		MacGillivray's Warbler	c	c	c	
c	c	c		Common Yellowthroat	c	c	c	
				Yellow-breasted Chat	r	r		
r	r	r		Wilson's Warbler		o	o	
r	r			American Redstart	o	o		
				Weaver Finches:				
r	r	r	r	House Sparrow	o	o	o	o

Blackbirds and Orioles:

				Species					
r		r		Bobolink	r	r	r		
lc	lc	lc		Western Meadowlark	lc	lc	lc		
lc	lc	lc		Yellow-headed Blackbird	lc	lc	lc		
c	c	c		Red-winged Blackbird	c	c	c		
	x			Tri-colored Blackbird					
r	r	r		Northern Oriole	r	r	r		
				Rusty Blackbird				x	
	x			Common Grackle					
c	c	c		Brewer's Blackbird	c	c	c		
o	o	o		Brown-headed Cowbird	o	o	o		

Tanagers:

				Species					
c	c	o		Western Tanager	c	c	r		

Grosbeaks, Sparrows and Finches:

				Species					
				Rose-breasted Grosbeak	x				
r		r		Black-headed Grosbeak	c	c			
				Indigo Bunting	x				
o	o			Lazuli Bunting	o	o			
o	o	o	o	Evening Grosbeak	o	r	r		o
c	c	c	o	Cassin's Finch	c	c	c		o
				House Finch		x			
o	o	o	o	Pine Grosbeak	o	o	o		o
r	r	r	o	Gray-crowned Rosy Finch	o		o		
o	o	o	r	Black Rosy Finch	c	c	o		
		r	r	Common Redpoll				r	r
a	a	a	o	Pine Siskin	c	o	c		
r	r	r		American Goldfinch	o	o	o		
o	o	o	r	Red Crossbill	o	o	o		r
x	x			White-winged Crossbill	x	x			
lc	lc	lc		Green-tailed Towhee	lc	lc	lc		
r	r			Rufous-sided Towhee	r	r			
o		o		Lark Bunting	r				
c	c	c		Savannah Sparrow	c	c	c		
r	r			Grasshopper Sparrow	o				
c	c	c		Vesper Sparrow	c	c	c		
o	o			Lark Sparrow	r	r			
a	a	c	o	Dark-eyed Junco	a	a	c		r
r		r	r	Tree Sparrow	r			r	r
c	c	c		Chipping Sparrow	c	c	c		
				Clay-colored Sparrow		r			
lc	lc	c		Brewer's Sparrow	c	c	c		
				Harris' Sparrow	x			x	
c	c	c		White-crowned Sparrow	a	a	a		
		r		White-throated Sparrow					r
r	r			Fox Sparrow	o	o			
o	o			Lincoln's Sparrow	o	o			r
c	c	c		Song Sparrow	c	c	c		
r	r			McCown's Longspur					
		o	o	Lapland Longspur					
		o	o	Snow Bunting				r	r

68

acknowledgements

I am indebted to a number of individuals who have assisted me during the preparation of this book.

Chief Park Naturalist Al Mebane, and Assistant Chief Park Naturalist John Tyers of Yellowstone took a very active interest in the book, and were most helpful in providing resources for the book.

Chief Park Naturalist Charles McCurdy of Grand Teton provided me with information on Grand Teton National Park and its birds. He also provided me with an invaluable list of resource persons.

Former Yellowstone Chief Park Naturalist Bill Dunmire, former Grand Teton Chief Park Naturalist Willard E. Dilley, former Yellowstone Assistant Chief Naturalist Stan Canter, former North District Naturalist Supervisor George Morrison, former Yellowstone Sub-district Naturalist Supervisor George Downing, and current North District Supervising Naturalist John Whitman were all kind enough to evaluate the manuscript and share their observations of birds in the two parks.

Botanist Don Despain, of the Yellowstone Biologists Office, provided invaluable assistance in writing habitat complex descriptions, and biologists Glenn Cole and Doug Houston, of the same office, read and evaluated the manuscript.

I am deeply indebted to Seasonal Naturalists Paul Schullery and Steve Gniadek of Yellowstone, and Cheryl McGinley of Grand Teton for their help in gathering information, providing records on bird observations, and evaluating the manuscript.

Illustrator Bill Chapman was most helpful in developing the book's format and design features, and the following people read and evaluated the manuscript or provided suggestions, ideas, or encouragement:

Don Arceneaux, Butch Bach, Gordon Bolander, Joanna Booser, Ila Bucknall, Douglas C. Campbell, Geri Hape, Chris Judson, Reed Kelly, Hugh Kingery, Charles Milliken, John and Judy O'Neale, Bert Raynes, Ed Riddell, Susan Sindt, and Robert Wood.

Finally, I wish to express my appreciation to my wife, Peggy, and my daughter, Jackie, for patiently reading or listening to, and passing judgment on hundreds of passages from the book, and for untold hours of typing and proofreading.

REFERENCES

Behle, William H. and Perry, Michael L. 1975. Utah Birds — A Guide, Check List and Occurrence Chart, Utah Museum of Natural History.

Bent, Arthur Cleveland. 1915-1968. Life Histories of North American Birds, Dover Publications, New York.

Binford, Laurence C. 1974. Birds of Western North America, MacMillan Publishing Co., New York.

Blackford, John L. 1956. Western Wonderlands, Vantage Press Inc., New York.

Brooks, Maurice. 1967. The Life of the Mountains, McGraw-Hill, Inc., New York.

Cameron, Angus and Parnall, Peter. 1971. The Nightwatchers, Four Winds Press, New York.

Davenport, Margaret B. December, 1974. Piscivorous Avifauna on Yellowstone Lake, U.S. National Park Service, Yellowstone National Park, Wyoming.

Despain, Don. 1974. Major Vegetational Zones of Yellowstone National Park, Information Paper No. 19, Yellowstone National Park Service, U.S. Department of the Interior.

Dilley, Willard E. Autumn and Winter, 1968. Birds of the Grand Tetons, The Naturalist Magazine, Volume 18.

Dixon, Joseph S. and Sumner, Lowell. 1953. Birds and Mammals of the Sierra Nevada, University of California Press, Berkeley.

Grant, Karen and Verne. 1968. Hummingbirds and Their Flowers, Columbia University Press.

Hall, Henry M. 1960. A Gathering of Shore Birds, Bramhall House, New York.

Harry, Bryan and Dilley, Willard E. 1964. Wildlife of Yellowstone and Grand Teton National Parks, Wheelwright Lithographic Co., Salt Lake.

Henrickson, William H. March, 1969. Plant Ecology Studies RSP 39, An Open-file Progress Report Reflecting Observations and Working Hypothesis for Future Study.

Ingersoll, Ernest. 1923. Birds in Legend, Fable and Folklore. Longmans, Green and Co., New York.

Johnsgard, Paul A. 1975. North American Game Birds, University of Nebraska Press, Lincoln.

Line, Les. (Editor). July, 1970. The Unknown Owl, Audubon Magazine, Volume 72, No. 4.

Livingston, John A. 1966. Birds of the Northern Forest, Houghton-Mifflin Co., Boston.

Lopez, Barry. May, 1975. Least in Strength—Mighty Chickadee—Strongest in Mind. National Wildlife Magazine, Volume 13, No. 3.

McDougall, W. B. and Baggley, Herma A. 1956. Plants of Yellowstone National Park, Yellowstone Library and Museum Association.

McElroy, Thomas P. Jr., 1974. The Habitat Guide to Birding, Alfred A. Knopf, Inc., New York.

Murie, Adolph. 1940. Ecology of the Coyote in Yellowstone, Fauna Series No. 1, Conservation Bulletin No. 4, U.S. Government Printing Office, Washington, D.C.

Pearson, T. Gilbert (Editor). 1917. Birds of America, Garden City Books, Garden City, New York.

Peterson, Roger T. 1961. A Field Guide to Western Birds, Houghton-Mifflin Co., Boston.

Robbins, Chandler S.; Bruun, Burtel; Zim, Herbert S. 1966. A Guide to Field Identification Birds of North America, Golden Press, New York.

Scharff, Robert (Editor). 1966. Yellowstone and Grand Teton National Parks, David McKay Co., Inc., New York.

Skinner, Milton P. 1925. Birds of Yellowstone National Park, Roosevelt Wildlife Bulletin, Volume 3, No. 1, Roosevelt Wildlife Forest Experiment Station of New York State College of Forestry at Syracuse University.

Stebbins, Cyril A. and Robert C. 1954. Birds of Yosemite National Park, Yosemite Natural History Association.

Swenson, Jon E. March, 1975. Ecology of the Bald Eagle and Osprey in Yellowstone National Park. Thesis submitted in partial fulfillment for degree of Master of Science, Montana State University.

Taylor, Dale L., July, 1974. Forest Fires in Yellowstone National Park, Journal of Forest History.

Walkinshaw, Lawrence. 1949. The Sandhill Crane, Bulletin No. 29, Cranbrook Institute of Science.

index

Field Notes